My
Stress
TRACKER

A JOURNAL TO HELP YOU MAP OUT AND MANAGE YOUR STRESS LEVELS

ANNA BARNES

MY STRESS TRACKER

An Hachette UK Company
www.hachette.co.uk

Vie Books, an imprint of Summersdale Publishers Ltd
Part of Octopus Publishing Group Limited
Carmelite House
50 Victoria Embankment
LONDON
EC4Y 0DZ

www.summersdale.com

Printed and bound in China

ISBN: 978-1-78783-533-7

Substantial discounts on bulk quantities of Summersdale books are available to corporations, professional associations and other organizations. For details contact general enquiries: telephone: +44 (0) 1243 771107 or email: enquiries@summersdale.com.

DISCLAIMER

THIS BOOK IS NOT INTENDED AS A SUBSTITUTE FOR THE MEDICAL ADVICE OF A DOCTOR. IF YOU ARE EXPERIENCING PROBLEMS WITH STRESS, IT IS ALWAYS BEST TO FOLLOW THE ADVICE OF A HEALTH PROFESSIONAL.

Within you there is a stillness and a sanctuary to which you can retreat at any time and be yourself.

HERMANN HESSE

Introduction

Stress is a part of life. When things don't go to plan, or when there's so much going on we can't keep up, it's completely natural to feel tense, irritable and wound up too tightly.

However, our lifestyles often mean that stress, which should be a short-term reaction, is prolonged. We get used to the feeling of being stressed and think of it as normal, sometimes feeling tense for so long that the exact cause is no longer clear.

Enter the stress tracker – a handy tool to help you map your emotions over time. Whether you want to understand what makes you feel stressed and why, or learn more about your mood patterns, this book has everything you need to see the bigger picture.

Document your stress levels every day with the monthly trackers, try the guided relaxation exercises, enjoy the puzzles (all answers on p.157–158) and use the spaces in this book to explore your feelings. Over time, a clear record will begin to emerge of you and your mind, which you can use to develop a deeper awareness of your stress and how to manage it.

Daily tracker

On each day this month, colour in the
shapes according to your stress rating.

KEY

◻ Very calm   ◻ Mostly calm   ◻ Calm
◻ Stressed   ◻ Very stressed

Why am I stressed?

Use this space to write down your thoughts
about how the past month has gone, and the
things that might be causing you stress.

Stress-busting tips

Identify triggers

Although there are plenty of things you can do in the moment to calm feelings of stress, the best way to help yourself in the long term is to understand what triggers those feelings in the first place. You may be able to point to big life events, such as moving house, beginning a new job or changes in your personal circumstances.

However, stress can just as easily come from smaller day-to-day things. Examine your regular patterns and keep track of when you feel agitated. Perhaps it's during certain parts of your day, such as your commute, or when you're facing your to-do list. Maybe it's when you're dealing with a particular person or place.

If you can't see any immediate cause, consider your lifestyle – your diet or a lack of sleep might be affecting your well-being, or perhaps you don't give yourself enough time to relax and unwind.

Of course, we are all complex individuals, so there may not be one simple answer. However, every day spent paying attention to how you are reacting to the world around you will help you to become more self-aware, and once you understand the roots of your stress, you can then take steps to deal with them.

Know your body

In your journey to understanding stress, it's important to learn how to listen to your body. Stress has a range of physical symptoms that can easily be ignored, so make sure you know what to look out for. Common symptoms can include feeling overwhelmed or irritable, having racing thoughts or difficulty concentrating, or experiencing headaches, dizziness, muscle tension, fatigue or changes in your appetite. Being able to spot these symptoms as an indication of stress is a vital step on the way to managing your stress and preventing it in the future.

Calm thoughts

Use this page to write down the good things that
people have said to you — compliments they have given,
or advice they have shared — and turn back to it
whenever you need a boost.

Calm activity

Complete this soothing sudoku, which uses the letters of the word **CALMER** instead of the numbers 1 to 6.

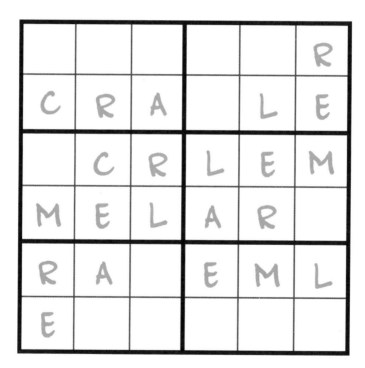

You'll find the answers on page 157.

4-7-8 Breathing

This is a simple breathing exercise to help reduce feelings of anxiety and stress, which can be done anywhere, any time.

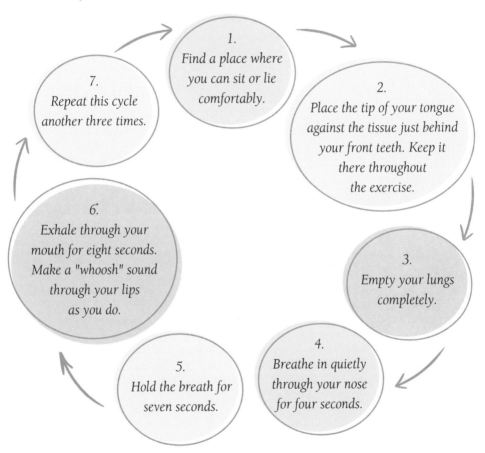

1.
Find a place where you can sit or lie comfortably.

2.
Place the tip of your tongue against the tissue just behind your front teeth. Keep it there throughout the exercise.

3.
Empty your lungs completely.

4.
Breathe in quietly through your nose for four seconds.

5.
Hold the breath for seven seconds.

6.
Exhale through your mouth for eight seconds. Make a "whoosh" sound through your lips as you do.

7.
Repeat this cycle another three times.

If you feel light-headed after trying this for the first time, stay sitting down while you wait for the feeling to pass.

If you can't hold your breath for the full seven seconds, try shorter intervals at first: breathe in for two seconds, hold for three seconds, and breathe out for four.

If you would like further support for this exercise, you can download apps which guide you through the technique.

Stress tracker

Use this page to log some of the moments when you have felt stressed this month. Record when it happened, why it happened, how stressful it was, and how you responded.

MOMENT:

CAUSE:

STRESS LEVEL (1-10):

RESPONSE:

MOMENT:

CAUSE:

STRESS LEVEL (1-10):

RESPONSE:

MOMENT:

CAUSE:

STRESS LEVEL (1-10):

RESPONSE:

YOU ARE NOT
YOUR STRESS

Colouring

Colour in the pattern on this page in whatever ways and colours you find soothing. Take pleasure in this slow, patient, peaceful activity.

Set peace of mind
as your highest goal,
and organize your
life around it.

BRIAN TRACY

Daily tracker

On each day this month, colour in the
shapes according to your stress rating.

KEY

- ☐ Very calm
- ☐ Mostly calm
- ☐ Calm
- ☐ Stressed
- ☐ Very stressed

Why am I stressed?

Use this space to write down your thoughts about how the past month has gone, and the things that might be causing you stress.

Stress-busting tips

Make time for self-care

Many of us leave little time for self-care in our day-to-day routines and tend to rush from one thing to the next without stopping. However, without sufficient time to unwind, we become stressed. To keep yourself feeling your best, be sure to make time for self-care in your day or week, even if you have to schedule it in. Have something that you do for you that will make you feel good, whether that's cooking a delicious meal, listening to music, phoning a friend, watching a film or going for a run.

Little chores

Self-care doesn't just mean treating yourself to the things that make you happy. It also means keeping up the little chores of day-to-day life, like brushing your teeth, doing the laundry and washing the dishes. It may seem insignificant or boring, but these small actions are a hugely valuable part of looking after yourself, and keeping up with them makes you feel calmer and more in control. If you are feeling stressed, set yourself the task of completing one tiny chore and see how much better you feel once it's done.

Say no

Our days can easily fill up with the things that we agree to do for other people, but there are negative effects to taking on more than you should, not least that it raises your stress levels. Next time you are asked to do an extra job, whether it's at work or at home, assess your schedule and decide whether you want to take it on, whether you have time to, and what effect it might have on your well-being. Don't be afraid to say "no" if you need to.

My tension
is melting
away

Calm activity

Count the pillows.

Attitude of gratitude

Feeling grateful for good things, moments or people in your
life is healthy for the mind and helps to de-stress the body.
List some of the things you're grateful for here and reflect
on each one and how it makes you feel.

THINGS I'M GRATEFUL FOR:

GREAT THINGS THAT HAPPENED TO ME RECENTLY:

PEOPLE I'M GRATEFUL FOR:

Colouring

Doodle to de-stress

Use this space to doodle. Imagine that any stress is leaving your body as you draw, travelling down your arm and out of your pen or pencil.

Stress tracker

Use this page to log some of the moments when you have felt stressed this month. Record when it happened, why it happened, how stressful it was, and how you responded.

MOMENT:

CAUSE:

STRESS LEVEL (1-10):

RESPONSE:

MOMENT:

CAUSE:

STRESS LEVEL (1-10):

RESPONSE:

MOMENT:

CAUSE:

STRESS LEVEL (1-10):

RESPONSE:

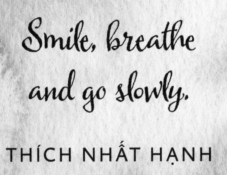

Smile, breathe
and go slowly.

THÍCH NHẤT HẠNH

Daily tracker

On each day this month, colour in the
shapes according to your stress rating.

KEY

- ☐ Very calm
- ☐ Mostly calm
- ☐ Calm
- ☐ Stressed
- ☐ Very stressed

Why am I stressed?

Use this space to write down your thoughts about how the past month has gone, and the things that might be causing you stress.

Stress-busting tips

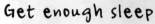

Get enough sleep

Sleep is the body's way of recharging itself, so it will probably be no surprise to hear that, to help minimize your stress levels, you need to get plenty of it. The average person should aim for eight hours of sleep a night, although some may find that they function better on more or slightly less. If you find getting to sleep challenging, try establishing a bedtime routine. Yours might involve having a bath or reading a book. Eventually, regular pre-bedtime activities will signal to your body and mind that it's time to switch off and go to sleep.

No screens

Another factor that determines how much we sleep is the amount of time we spend staring at a screen. Phones, tablets, computers and TVs all give out blue light which interrupts your natural sleep/wake cycle and makes your body think that it's time to be awake and alert. This leads not only to less sleep, but to lower-quality sleep, so even if you do get your eight hours, you could still wake up feeling tired and therefore more prone to stress. There are apps you can download to help counter the blue light, but to allow yourself to properly prepare for sleep, try to avoid looking at screens for at least 30 minutes, if not an hour, before bed.

Bedroom haven

For restful sleep, it can help to make your bedroom a sanctuary. It should be somewhere that you want to be in, so keep it clean, tidy and clutter free. Opt for soft lighting to give the room a warm glow, or try scented oils to further create a relaxing atmosphere. Lavender, chamomile, jasmine and vanilla are all believed to promote restful sleep. Most importantly, try not to use your bedroom for anything other than sleep or sex, so that it's a place that you associate with bedtime only.

Calm activity

Find the following in the
word search below:

Bedtime * Sleep * Shut-eye * Relax
Slumber * Forty winks

S	K	N	I	W	Y	T	R	O	F	P	T
L	K	J	H	G	F	D	S	E	T	R	S
P	O	U	Y	U	T	S	L	E	E	P	L
A	E	N	H	U	R	H	V	Q	T	S	A
T	F	M	O	F	C	U	X	S	S	Q	V
M	W	E	I	R	U	T	K	N	L	M	C
H	F	L	N	T	F	E	G	Y	U	P	Z
Q	U	F	V	C	D	Y	E	W	M	A	S
L	T	R	E	S	X	E	U	Q	B	Z	W
P	Q	Y	R	D	V	B	B	O	E	J	U
R	E	L	A	X	Q	K	S	N	R	O	P
C	H	V	E	W	I	H	V	L	M	U	X

You'll find the answers on page 157.

Meditation

Meditation is the art of allowing your mind to become completely still, like a pool of water with no ripples. It's a great skill to learn to help you cope with feelings of stress, and even just five minutes of stillness and calm breathing can make you feel better. Here's how to get started:

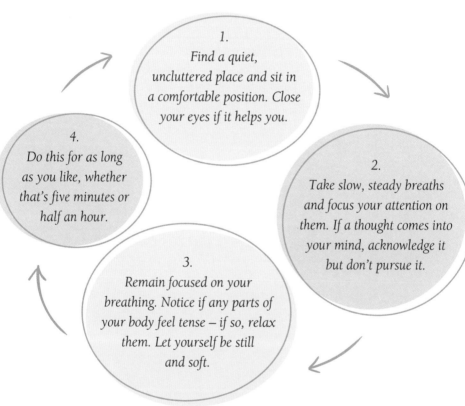

1.
Find a quiet, uncluttered place and sit in a comfortable position. Close your eyes if it helps you.

2.
Take slow, steady breaths and focus your attention on them. If a thought comes into your mind, acknowledge it but don't pursue it.

3.
Remain focused on your breathing. Notice if any parts of your body feel tense – if so, relax them. Let yourself be still and soft.

4.
Do this for as long as you like, whether that's five minutes or half an hour.

Emptying your mind is easier said than done, and some people find it easier to reach that state of calm than others. However, with practice, anybody can master meditation and reap the benefits.

Calm thoughts

Use this page to write down the good things that
people have said to you — compliments they have given,
or advice they have shared — and turn back to it
whenever you need a boost.

Stress tracker

Use this page to log some of the moments when you have felt stressed this month. Record when it happened, why it happened, how stressful it was, and how you responded.

MOMENT:

CAUSE:

STRESS LEVEL (1-10):

RESPONSE:

MOMENT:

CAUSE:

STRESS LEVEL (1-10):

RESPONSE:

MOMENT:

CAUSE:

STRESS LEVEL (1-10):

RESPONSE:

Colouring

Tension is who you
think you should be.
Relaxation is
who you are.

CHINESE PROVERB

Daily tracker

On each day this month, colour in the
shapes according to your stress rating.

KEY

- ☐ Very calm
- ☐ Mostly calm
- ☐ Calm
- ☐ Stressed
- ☐ Very stressed

Why am I stressed?

Use this space to write down your thoughts about how the past month has gone, and the things that might be causing you stress.

Stress-busting tips

Good food, good mood

Your diet is another important factor in helping you feel calm, and eating the right things can have a hugely positive effect on your mood. Eating three meals a day at regularly spaced intervals will maintain your blood sugar levels and keep you from feeling hungry and irritable. Eating at least five portions of fruit and vegetables a day is important too, as these will give you the right vitamins to help your brain function at its best. You don't have to overhaul your whole lifestyle at once, but making small, healthy choices every day can go a long way to making you feel calmer and happier.

Healthy fats

Not all fats are bad news. We all need to consume enough healthy fats to keep our brains functioning properly, and research has found that those who cut out all types of fat can suffer from symptoms of anxiety and depression. Of the four types of fat, the unhealthy varieties are saturated fats (found in certain meats and dairy products, and, to a lesser degree, eggs) and trans fats (mainly found in fried and baked foods). These two types should be consumed in moderation. However, polyunsaturated fats – found in walnuts, peanuts, sesame and sunflower seeds, olive oil and oily fish – are vital in maintaining a healthy brain, and monounsaturated fats – found in nuts, olives and avocados – are rich in vitamin E which can help to lower cholesterol.

I WILL NOURISH IN
ORDER TO FLOURISH

Calm activity

Put your finger on the dot and guide
yourself to the pillow.

You'll find the answers on page 157.

Attitude of gratitude

Feeling grateful for good things, moments or people in your
life is healthy for the mind and helps to de-stress the body.
List some of the things you're grateful for here and reflect
on each one and how it makes you feel.

THINGS I'M GRATEFUL FOR:

GREAT THINGS THAT HAPPENED TO ME RECENTLY:

PEOPLE I'M GRATEFUL FOR:

Doodle to de-stress

Stress tracker

Use this page to log some of the moments when you have felt stressed this month. Record when it happened, why it happened, how stressful it was, and how you responded.

MOMENT:

CAUSE:

STRESS LEVEL (1-10):

RESPONSE:

MOMENT:

CAUSE:

STRESS LEVEL (1-10):

RESPONSE:

MOMENT:

CAUSE:

STRESS LEVEL (1-10):

RESPONSE:

Learn to be calm
and you will
always be happy.

PARAMAHANSA YOGANANDA

I breathe in
peace, I breathe
out stress

Daily tracker

On each day this month, colour in the
shapes according to your stress rating.

KEY

☐ Very calm   ☐ Mostly calm   ☐ Calm
☐ Stressed   ☐ Very stressed

Why am I stressed?

Use this space to write down your thoughts about how the past month has gone, and the things that might be causing you stress.

Stress-busting tips

Pep up with protein

It's important to eat enough protein, particularly during stressful periods. Protein helps your brain to absorb tryptophan, which then helps to produce serotonin, a hormone crucial for regulating your mood, among other things. Tryptophan- and protein-rich foods include chicken, lamb, fish, soya beans and many nuts and seeds. Walnuts, flaxseeds, pumpkin seeds and sunflower seeds are a particularly good source of tryptophan; sprinkle them on salads or, if you're not a big fan, use a coffee grinder to reduce them to a fine powder and add the mixture to soups and stews.

Watch your drinks

When you're feeling stressed, try cutting down on tea and coffee. Caffeine is a stimulant, so it will increase any anxiety or tension that you may be feeling. Alcohol, on the other hand, is a depressant, which tends to alter or exaggerate your current state of mind. So, if you're already feeling tense, instead of helping you to relax there's a chance that your favourite drink could have the opposite effect and aggravate your symptoms.

Go green

If you're looking for a calming drink, try green tea. As well as containing much lower levels of caffeine than black tea, green tea also contains the amino acid L-theanine, which has been found to have calming effects. Many also claim that it's a good anti-anxiety remedy. If you don't like the taste of straight green tea, why not try one of the many variants on the market? Green teas are available in a multitude of flavours, including strawberry, mandarin, echinacea (good for warding off colds), mint, ginseng and nettle.

Calm activity

Unscramble the following words to find different kinds of tea:

1. LOGONO

2. AKBASFTRE

3. AMAHCT

4. GARLEERY

5. ELOMAMIC

You'll find the answers on page 157.

Progressive relaxation

You carry stress in your body as well as your mind. When you're anxious, your muscles will tense up — often without you realizing. Progressive relaxation is a good way to release this tension.

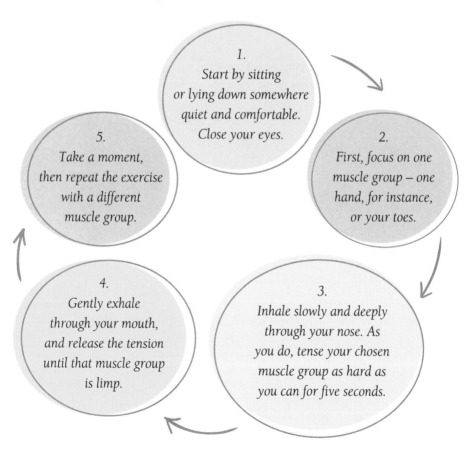

1.
Start by sitting or lying down somewhere quiet and comfortable. Close your eyes.

2.
First, focus on one muscle group – one hand, for instance, or your toes.

3.
Inhale slowly and deeply through your nose. As you do, tense your chosen muscle group as hard as you can for five seconds.

4.
Gently exhale through your mouth, and release the tension until that muscle group is limp.

5.
Take a moment, then repeat the exercise with a different muscle group.

Continue this process until you have covered all the muscle groups in your body; it should help you to feel calmer and more peaceful.

LET GO OF THE
THINGS YOU
CAN'T CONTROL

Calm thoughts

Use this page to write down the good things that
people have said to you — compliments they have given,
or advice they have shared — and turn back to it
whenever you need a boost.

Colouring

Stress tracker

Use this page to log some of the moments when you have felt stressed this month. Record when it happened, why it happened, how stressful it was, and how you responded.

MOMENT:

CAUSE:

STRESS LEVEL (1-10):

RESPONSE:

MOMENT:

CAUSE:

STRESS LEVEL (1-10):

RESPONSE:

MOMENT:

CAUSE:

STRESS LEVEL (1-10):

RESPONSE:

Doodle to de-stress

Daily tracker

On each day this month, colour in the shapes according to your stress rating.

KEY

- ☐ Very calm
- ☐ Mostly calm
- ☐ Calm
- ☐ Stressed
- ☐ Very stressed

Why am I stressed?

Use this space to write down your thoughts about how the past month has gone, and the things that might be causing you stress.

Stress-busting tips

Get moving!

Exercise is not only good for your body – it's good for your mind too! Getting outside and moving your body releases serotonin, which is both a mood booster and a stress buster. Even something as simple as walking is beneficial and easy to incorporate into your day. Try walking to work or taking a 20-minute stroll in your lunch break, for instance. However you choose to move, being more active will help you to relax in your downtime, sleep better and increase positivity, all of which will ultimately help you feel calmer and stay on top of your stress levels.

Take the plunge

If you want to be peaceful as you exercise, then try swimming. As you move through the water you will fall into a soothing rhythm, which can help to lull yourself into a calmer mindset. If you're feeling adventurous, you could even try wild swimming: that's swimming outdoors. The cold water invigorates you and can even give you a natural high. Swimming outdoors and engaging with nature as you swim has also been shown to improve your mood.

Buddy up

If you find it hard to motivate yourself to exercise, then try teaming up with a friend. It's easier to keep up a habit – and is much more fun – when you have someone else by your side who is sharing your experience. If the social aspect appeals, then you could also join a class or a club. Yoga, Zumba, dance classes, running clubs, sports teams – the possibilities are almost endless, and will all get you moving and feeling good.

I am relaxed
and I am calm

Calm activity

Create as many words as you can from the following letters, and see if you can find the calm seven-letter word.

E N I R S T G

You'll find the answer on page 157.

Attitude of gratitude

Feeling grateful for good things, moments or people in your life is healthy for the mind and helps to de-stress the body. List some of the things you're grateful for here and reflect on each one and how it makes you feel.

THINGS I'M GRATEFUL FOR:

GREAT THINGS THAT HAPPENED TO ME RECENTLY:

PEOPLE I'M GRATEFUL FOR:

Stress tracker

Use this page to log some of the moments when you have felt stressed this month. Record when it happened, why it happened, how stressful it was, and how you responded.

MOMENT:

CAUSE:

STRESS LEVEL (1-10):

RESPONSE:

MOMENT:

CAUSE:

STRESS LEVEL (1-10):

RESPONSE:

MOMENT:

CAUSE:

STRESS LEVEL (1-10):

RESPONSE:

Notes

Use this space to reflect on your
de-stressing journey so far.

When something feels
heavy, break it down
until one piece of it is
light enough to handle.
Begin there.

BERNIE SIEGEL

Doodle to de-stress

Daily tracker

On each day this month, colour in the
shapes according to your stress rating.

KEY

○ Very calm   ○ Mostly calm   ○ Calm

○ Stressed   ○ Very stressed

18

17

19

21

20

22

23

24

25

28   26

27

29

31   30

Why am I stressed?

Use this space to write down your thoughts about how the past month has gone, and the things that might be causing you stress.

Stress-busting tips

Laugh out loud

Laughter is the best medicine, or so the saying goes… but it's true! And it might just be one of the best ways to combat feelings of stress. Laughter relaxes your body, gives your immune system a boost, increases blood flow – and it triggers the release of endorphins, the chemicals that make you feel good. So tune in to some comedy or have a good giggle with a friend to give yourself a well-deserved boost.

Just connect

When you're stressed it's easy to close in on yourself, pushing yourself to keep working harder. Letting your hair down might feel like the last thing you should do, but actually the times when you're stressed are probably the times when you most need social connection. Use meet-ups with friends to talk about what's on your mind, or allow them to be a distraction from your worries. People who are socially connected are happier and healthier, so keep your friends close during hard times and let them support you.

Go outside

To help keep your stress levels in check, make sure to get plenty of fresh air. Whether it's a walk around the block or a lunch break spent in your local park, getting some lungfuls of fresh, outdoor air can do wonders for your mood. Not only does it reduce stress and calm the mind, it restores energy, strengthens your immune system and can sharpen your focus. Even just twenty minutes outdoors can make you feel calmer and happier.

Calm activity

Find the unlit candle.

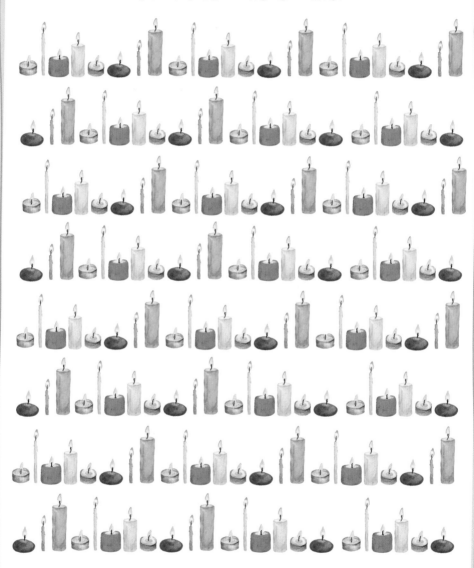

You'll find the answers on page 157.

Calm thoughts

Use this page to write down the good things that people have said to you — compliments they have given, or advice they have shared — and turn back to it whenever you need a boost.

Stress tracker

Use this page to log some of the moments when you have felt stressed this month. Record when it happened, why it happened, how stressful it was, and how you responded.

MOMENT:

CAUSE:

STRESS LEVEL (1-10):

RESPONSE:

MOMENT:

CAUSE:

STRESS LEVEL (1-10):

RESPONSE:

MOMENT:

CAUSE:

STRESS LEVEL (1-10):

RESPONSE:

Get your blood pumping

If you're feeling tense and tightly wound, sometimes the best antidote is vigorous exercise. Here are some options:

Try running. Whether you go for a ten-minute sprint or for a longer, steadier run, grabbing your trainers and pounding the pavement is a fantastic way to get tension out of your system.

HIIT – high intensity interval training – is great for burning energy fast. These cardio workouts are typically only 15–20 minutes long but, during this time, you push yourself to the max with intense bursts of activity. Look for classes in your local gym, or search for videos online.

Kick-boxing is a blend of martial arts and boxing, and it's an incredible way to release your energy. As well as giving you the chance to channel your pent-up stress into a punching bag, it also teaches you breathing techniques and can help to boost your confidence.

Any exercise that gets your heart rate going and your blood pumping will be an amazing stress buster. Experiment with a range of sports and activities until you find one that works for you.

Note: Before starting any kind of exercise, be sure to warm up your body first to protect yourself against injury.

Colouring

*Let your soul stand
cool and composed before
a million universes.*

WALT WHITMAN

Daily tracker

On each day this month, colour in the
shapes according to your stress rating.

KEY

☐ Very calm   ☐ Mostly calm   ☐ Calm
☐ Stressed   ☐ Very stressed

Why am I stressed?

Use this space to write down your thoughts about how the past month has gone, and the things that might be causing you stress.

Stress-busting tips

Find positives in negatives

Coping with stress can often be down to how you are able to handle different situations. When something difficult or unexpected happens, it's a natural reaction to feel tense or to let negative feelings take over. Next time this happens, try to find a positive. This can be hard at first, especially in situations that have a strong and lasting effect on your life. But finding even a small positive is the first step to feeling better. Perhaps you've lost your job; the positive is that now you can retrain for the career you've always wanted. Maybe a relationship has ended; the positive here is that now you're free to find someone more suited to you. Finding the silver lining is not always an easy thing to do, but it's a skill that will greatly help you to remain calm and collected.

Step back

When we're facing a problem, it often feels like the be-all and end-all, and it's easy for everything else in life to become eclipsed. If you're feeling this way, try taking a step back and looking at the bigger picture. Ask yourself if what you're stressed about will matter in a week, a month or a year. Quite often, the answer is no. Adjusting your perspective in this way can help to take the edge off the things that are troubling you right now.

I am letting
go of my
worries

Calm activity

Complete this soothing sudoku, which uses the letters of the word **STEADY** instead of the numbers 1 to 6.

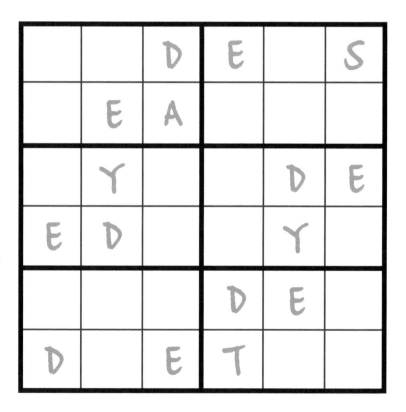

You'll find the answers on page 158.

Attitude of gratitude

Feeling grateful for good things, moments or people in your life is healthy for the mind and helps to de-stress the body. List some of the things you're grateful for here and reflect on each one and how it makes you feel.

THINGS I'M GRATEFUL FOR:

GREAT THINGS THAT HAPPENED TO ME RECENTLY:

PEOPLE I'M GRATEFUL FOR:

Stress tracker

Use this page to log some of the moments when you have felt stressed this month. Record when it happened, why it happened, how stressful it was, and how you responded.

MOMENT:

CAUSE:

STRESS LEVEL (1-10):

RESPONSE:

MOMENT:

CAUSE:

STRESS LEVEL (1-10):

RESPONSE:

MOMENT:

CAUSE:

STRESS LEVEL (1-10):

RESPONSE:

Doodle to de-stress

Colouring

Notes

Use this space to jot down any goals or intentions you
have as you make progress on your de-stressing journey.

Daily tracker

On each day this month, colour in the
shapes according to your stress rating.

KEY

○ Very calm   ○ Mostly calm   ○ Calm
   ○ Stressed   ○ Very stressed

Why am I stressed?

Use this space to write down your thoughts about how the past month has gone, and the things that might be causing you stress.

Stress-busting tips

Just one thing

If your to-do list is making you feel overwhelmed, choose one thing to do and focus your whole attention on it. Ignore any interruptions – whether that's by turning off email notifications, switching off your phone or taking yourself into another room. No matter how many other things you have to do, don't begin another task until you've finished what you started. By giving yourself space and time, and by completing the job, you will regain your sense of control.

Stretch

Something as simple as stretching for 30 seconds can be a really effective stress-buster. Performing regular stretches helps to relieve muscle tension and it's excellent for your circulation.

Try a shoulder stretch: raise your arms above your head, lock your fingers and turn your palms so they're facing upward. Try to stretch your hands up while keeping your shoulders down. Hold this for a few breaths before bringing your hands down again.

Or try a stretch to open your chest. Stand up with your feet hip-width apart and look straight ahead. Clasp your hands behind you and then lift them as high as you can. If you spend a lot of time at a computer or desk, this stretch counteracts the effects of hunching over.

Write it out

We've all experienced racing thoughts – when it feels like your mind is on fast-forward, and that it's trying to hold on to too many things at once. Next time you feel like this, try putting pen to paper. Write a to-do list, so that all the jobs you keep remembering are not forgotten, or write a journal entry to channel and express your feelings. Writing is therapeutic, as it helps put a little distance between you and your thoughts, giving you space to find calm.

Calm activity

Find "calm".

```
Z O G V E M A C S C K R C X L
N X C A G L P J V M D J J R Q
W W K W E A N B I S A I K B W
N W V A L C L K S Q B G L Z P
Z K W W M A W V H T G Z G H Z
A H R Q B S B N L M M K O G X
E G H P C A S R Z Z F Y W O A
L P B M L A P V R Y I L N P A
A J P N M S Y T A C S R T X P
C A L S X U W U J K A J M S M
H A T A T T D C A O L F M J M
L M K P H V X Q O X I U I I H
F A M L W Z F K F S Y U P J W
L K T N L A G M O X F K I G Q
I F T U E C F L L W A C K N X
```

You'll find the answer on page 158.

Let it out

When you feel overwhelmed, sometimes the only way to deal with your emotion is to let it out — so don't hold back!

Cry: crying is a healthy and natural reaction to stress, helping you to release tension and cleansing the body of toxins and stress hormones. Lock the door and let yourself cry until you feel ready to face the world again.

Shout: scream, shout, make a noise! Let out your frustration in the most satisfying and immediate way possible. If you're worried about your neighbours, scream into a pillow to muffle the sound.

Sing: singing lowers the levels of cortisol in your body, and releases endorphins (feel-good chemicals), so pick your favourite song and belt it out at the top of your lungs.

Calm thoughts

Use this page to write down the good things that
people have said to you — compliments they have given,
or advice they have shared — and turn back to it
whenever you need a boost.

Colouring

Doodle to de-stress

Stress tracker

Use this page to log some of the moments when you have felt stressed this month. Record when it happened, why it happened, how stressful it was, and how you responded.

MOMENT:

CAUSE:

STRESS LEVEL (1-10):

RESPONSE:

MOMENT:

CAUSE:

STRESS LEVEL (1-10):

RESPONSE:

MOMENT:

CAUSE:

STRESS LEVEL (1-10):

RESPONSE:

*To the mind that
is still, the whole
universe surrenders.*

LAO TZU

Daily tracker

On each day this month, colour in the
shapes according to your stress rating.

KEY

- Very calm
- Mostly calm
- Calm
- Stressed
- Very stressed

Why am I stressed?

Use this space to write down your thoughts about how the past month has gone, and the things that might be causing you stress.

Stress-busting tips

Social media stress

Social media is a huge part of modern life but, despite all its benefits, it can leave us feeling unhappy and stressed. One of the main reasons for this is the way it encourages comparison. When your feed is filled with the accomplishments of other people it's easy to look at your own life against theirs and assume that everyone else is more beautiful or successful than you. The key thing to remember is that social media is a highlight reel and what you see is usually only the polished, curated version of a life. If you can use social media with this in mind, it relieves some of the pressure.

Curate positivity

Using social media can be stressful simply because of the content we see, so edit your feeds so that they only show you things that bring you joy. Follow positive accounts that you're interested in, unfollow the people who make you feel bad, and mute hashtags that make you feel sad, anxious or angry. Your social media accounts are your very own space, so take time to personalize them and make them a place that you are happy to spend time in.

Phone-free

Some studies show that many of us spend a seventh of our waking lives on social media, and there is mounting evidence that using these apps can be linked to anxiety, depression and higher stress levels. To look after your well-being, try limiting your time on social media. You could have a phone-free evening, for instance, or allow yourself only 30 minutes a day to check your accounts. It may be hard to do at first, but spending time offline is one of the simplest small changes you can make to improve your mental wellness.

I am centred,
and my mind
is becoming still

Calm activity

Put your finger on the dot and guide yourself to the pillow.

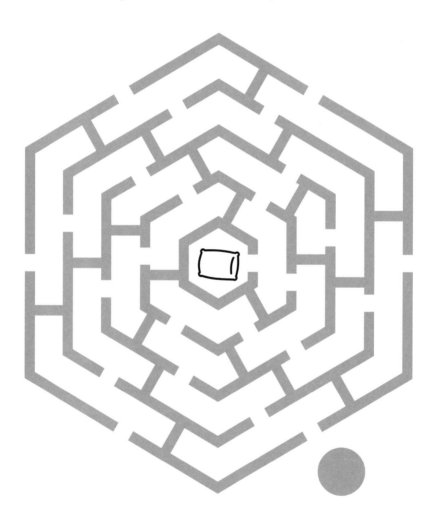

You'll find the answer on page 158.

Attitude of gratitude

Feeling grateful for good things, moments or people in your
life is healthy for the mind and helps to de-stress the body.
List some of the things you're grateful for here and reflect
on each one and how it makes you feel.

THINGS I'M GRATEFUL FOR:

GREAT THINGS THAT HAPPENED TO ME RECENTLY:

PEOPLE I'M GRATEFUL FOR:

STORMS DON'T
LAST FOREVER

Doodle to de-stress

Stress tracker

Use this page to log some of the moments when you have felt stressed this month. Record when it happened, why it happened, how stressful it was, and how you responded.

MOMENT:

CAUSE:

STRESS LEVEL (1-10):

RESPONSE:

MOMENT:

CAUSE:

STRESS LEVEL (1-10):

RESPONSE:

MOMENT:

CAUSE:

STRESS LEVEL (1-10):

RESPONSE:

Notes

Use this space to record any major insights, lessons
or breakthroughs on your de-stressing journey.

Daily tracker

On each day this month, colour in the
shapes according to your stress rating.

KEY

- ☐ Very calm
- ☐ Mostly calm
- ☐ Calm
- ☐ Stressed
- ☐ Very stressed

Why am I stressed?

Use this space to write down your thoughts
about how the past month has gone, and the
things that might be causing you stress.

Stress-busting tips

Tidy house, tidy mind

If you're feeling stressed, have a look at the space around you. Is it tidy and clean, or is it messy and disorganized? Studies have shown a link between tidier living spaces and a happier outlook, so for peace of mind, try tidying up. There's no need to deep clean the house every weekend; even small tidying sessions can improve the way you feel. Take an extra 30 seconds to wipe down the counter or the hob after cooking or always make your bed before you leave the house. Getting into the habit of doing these tiny acts will keep your home neat around the edges and keep you feeling comfortable and relaxed.

Home haven

Your home is your sanctuary. It's where you come at the end of every day to unwind, relax and to be yourself – so make sure that it's a place that you love. Choose your favourite colours and styles when you decorate to make it your own, and consider installing mood lighting to give your home ambience. Even if you can't decorate the walls or choose the furniture, you can still create an atmosphere that you love by bringing your favourite patterns and trends into your home with materials and ornaments.

Tackle money matters

If money worries are weighing on your mind, taking back control of the matter is the first step. Create a spreadsheet showing all your monthly outgoings and don't miss anything out. Then go over areas where you could save money. Do you have the best possible energy tariff, for example? Research this using price comparison sites to work out how your prices compare to others. And how much food do you throw away each week? If this is a problem, plan your meals for a week before you shop, to minimize waste.

Calm thoughts

Use this page to write down the good things that people have said to you — compliments they have given, or advice they have shared — and turn back to it whenever you need a boost.

Calm activity

Create as many words as you can from the following letters, and see if you can find the calm seven-letter word.

LRXAEDE

You'll find the answer on page 158.

Yoga

Try some simple yoga stretches or sequences.
It combines elements of meditation, stretching
and gentle exercise, so it's an activity that both
strengthens your body and calms your mind. Hold each
pose for 30 seconds, or as long as feels comfortable.

Child's Pose:
Sit back on your heels and lay your arms by
your sides, or stretch
them forward as far
as is comfortable.

Warrior 1:
Step one leg back until you are
in a lunge position. Keep your
front foot facing forward
and turn your back foot out
so it is at a right angle to
your body. Reach both arms
up to the sky, keeping your
neck long and your
shoulders soft.

Downward-Facing Dog:
With hands and feet on the floor,
push your hips toward the sky and
your heels toward the ground.
Feel the stretch in
your arms and
down your spine
and the back
of your legs.

Upward-Facing Dog:
Lie flat on your stomach. Place your hands either side
of your body and push your torso up until your arms
are straight. Soften your shoulders and roll them back
and down. Tilt your head and chest upward if you
can. Feel the stretch down your front.

Doodle to de-stress

Stress tracker

Use this page to log some of the moments when you have felt stressed this month. Record when it happened, why it happened, how stressful it was, and how you responded.

MOMENT:

CAUSE:

STRESS LEVEL (1-10):

RESPONSE:

MOMENT:

CAUSE:

STRESS LEVEL (1-10):

RESPONSE:

MOMENT:

CAUSE:

STRESS LEVEL (1-10):

RESPONSE:

Adopt the pace of nature:
her secret is patience.

RALPH WALDO EMERSON

Notes

Use this space to reflect on your de-stressing journey up to this point.

Daily tracker

On each day this month, colour in the
shapes according to your stress rating.

KEY

◯ Very calm ◯ Mostly calm ◯ Calm
◯ Stressed ◯ Very stressed

Why am I stressed?

Use this space to write down your thoughts about how the past month has gone, and the things that might be causing you stress.

Stress-busting tips

Open up

If you are struggling with stress and you're having trouble coping, don't bottle it up. Talk to a friend or family member about how you're feeling, or phone a helpline if you would prefer to speak anonymously. Opening up about how you feel can be incredibly challenging, but talking about what you're going through can make you feel better, and can help you to cope with the things you are facing.

Join a support group

If a particular situation is causing you to feel stressed, consider joining a support group. Studies have shown that talking to someone in the same situation as you, and who is in a similar emotional state, can help to ease the burden. Many people also find that support groups are a good midpoint between professional help and the emotional support of friends and family, who may not quite understand the experience you are going through. There may be a support group in your local area that's right for you, but if you can't find one there are many online support communities that you can seek out.

Professional support

If your stress is affecting your daily life, it could be time to seek professional help. Go to your doctor first and see what they suggest. They may recommend seeing a therapist, cognitive behavioural therapy, or even medication. Remember to be honest with your doctor – give as much detail as possible, and try not to hold back – and they'll be able to suggest the right solution for you. Whether or not to seek medical advice can be a challenging decision to make, but realizing and acknowledging that you need help is one of the biggest steps you can take toward feeling better.

This feeling
of stress
will pass

Calm activity

Unscramble the letters below to find calming words.

AILQTURN

NEERES

LETSNISSL

MOODSPEC

GINOHOST

You'll find the answers on page 158.

Attitude of gratitude

Feeling grateful for good things, moments or people in your life is healthy for the mind and helps to de-stress the body. List some of the things you're grateful for here and reflect on each one and how it makes you feel.

THINGS I'M GRATEFUL FOR:

GREAT THINGS THAT HAPPENED TO ME RECENTLY:

PEOPLE I'M GRATEFUL FOR:

Colouring

Calm activity

Complete this soothing sudoku, which uses the letters of the word PLACID instead of the numbers 1 to 6.

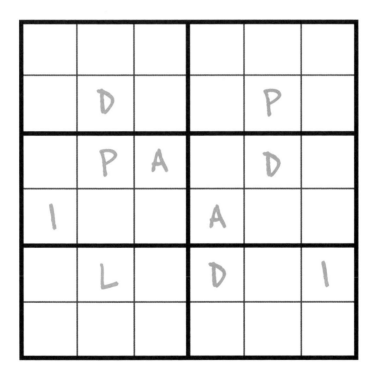

You'll find the answers on page 158.

Stress tracker

Use this page to log some of the moments when you have felt stressed this month. Record when it happened, why it happened, how stressful it was, and how you responded.

MOMENT:

CAUSE:

STRESS LEVEL (1-10):

RESPONSE:

MOMENT:

CAUSE:

STRESS LEVEL (1-10):

RESPONSE:

MOMENT:

CAUSE:

STRESS LEVEL (1-10):

RESPONSE:

Wherever you are,
be all there.

JIM ELLIOT

I am calm.
I am confident.
I am capable.

Conclusion

Congratulations — you've now tracked your stress for a whole year!

Now that you've reached the end of this book, take a look back over the last 12 months to see your journey. What does it show you? What have you learned? How do you want to continue?

Even a few minutes a day spent reflecting on your mood and taking note of how you feel can help you to be more in tune with yourself. Hopefully this book has given you space to reflect, and has provided you with insight, so that you can now continue your journey with a better understanding of your moods.

Doodle to de-stress

Notes

Notes

Calm activity answers

p.12

L	M	E	C	A	R
C	R	A	M	L	E
A	C	R	L	E	M
M	E	L	A	R	C
R	A	C	E	M	L
E	L	M	R	C	A

p.35

S	K	N	I	W	Y	T	R	O	F	P	T
L	K	J	H	G	F	D	S	E	T	R	S
P	O	U	Y	U	T	S	L	E	E	P	L
A	E	N	H	U	R	H	V	Q	T	S	A
T	F	M	O	F	C	U	X	S	S	Q	V
M	W	E	I	R	U	T	K	N	L	M	C
H	F	L	N	T	F	E	G	Y	U	P	Z
Q	U	F	V	C	D	Y	E	W	M	A	S
L	T	R	E	S	X	E	U	Q	B	Z	W
P	Q	Y	R	D	V	B	B	O	E	J	U
R	E	L	A	X	Q	K	S	N	R	O	P
C	H	V	E	W	I	H	V	L	M	U	X

p.48

p.59
1. Oolong
2. Breakfast
3. Matcha
4. Earl grey
5. Camomile

p.72 The seven-letter word is **RESTING**.

p.84

p.96

Y	T	D	E	A	S
S	E	A	Y	T	D
A	Y	T	S	D	E
E	D	S	A	Y	T
T	S	Y	D	E	A
D	A	E	T	S	Y

p.132 The seven-letter word is RELAXED.

p.144 1. tranquil

2. serene

3. stillness

4. composed

5. soothing

p.107

```
Z O G V E M A C S C K R C X L
N X C O G L P J V M D J J R Q
W W K W E A N B I S A I K B W
N W V A O C L K S Q B G L Z P
Z K W W M A W V H T G Z G H Z
A H R Q B S B N L P M K O G X
E G H P X A S R Z Z F Y W O A
Z P B P L A P V R Y I L N P A
R J P N Q S Y T A I S R T X P
C K G S X U W U J K A J M S M
H H T A T T D C J O Y F M J M
U M K P H V X Q O X I U I I H
F A M J W Z F K F S Y U P J W
L K T N L W G M O X F K I G Q
I F T U E C F L L W D C K N X
```

p.147

P	A	L	C	I	D
C	D	I	L	P	A
L	P	A	I	D	C
I	C	D	A	L	P
A	L	P	D	C	I
D	I	C	P	A	L

p.120

Image credits

Have you enjoyed this book?
If so, why not write a review on
your favourite website?

If you're interested in finding out more about
our books, find us on Facebook at Summersdale
Publishers, on Twitter at @Summersdale and
on Instagram at @summersdalebooks and get
in touch. We'd love to hear from you!

Thanks very much for buying this
Summersdale book.

www.summersdale.com